# The Kitchen Companion, Containing Valuable Recipes for Ice Creams, Puddings, Pies, Cakes, Blanc Mange, Custards, &c., &c., Being and Excellant Guide to the Housewife

# THE

# KITCHEN

6343

## Companion,

### CONTAINING VALUABLE RECIPES FOR

Ice Creams, Puddings, Pies, Cakes, Blanc
Mange, Custards, &c., &c.,

### BEING AN EXCELLENT GUIDE TO

## THE HOUSEWIFE.

BY

# RICHARDS, WARREN & FLINT BROTHERS.

### PHILADELPHIA.

# INTRODUCTION.

There being Drawing-Room Companions, Ladies' Companions, Floral Companions, Parlor Companions, &c., the idea was conceived that the Kitchen should not be neglected in this respect, and to fill the deficiency this little book is offered to the public as a "Kitchen Companion." Hoping it may be appreciated as its merits deserve, we leave it in your hands.

THE AUTHOR.

# Home.

There are few things which concern a community more than the preparation of the food upon which the people depend for life, health and comfort, and it is a gratifying fact that science in its onward march is placing within the reach of all the means by which the average of human happiness may be much enhanced each year, simply by the rendering of our daily fare more acceptable, and it is indeed a great consolation that we may have good dinners oftener than heretofore, for it is an admitted fact that the sympathies of men are more readily reached through their stomachs than any other way; it has been said that if you wish to ask a favor of any one select a time just after a good meal has been partaken, and no doubt the better the meal the more readily will the favor be granted (Wives who have not learned this fact by experience should make a note of it). The idea has been set forth and cherished, that the husband and the children are entitled to as much consideration as occasional guests, and the meals should be as tempting to the appetite, and the table ought to be set out as carefully and neatly every day as on special occasions. A gentleman whose better-half had not adopted this as her rule, played off a rich joke upon her one day. He addressed her a note, politely in-

forming her that a gentleman of her acquaintance—an old and true friend—would dine with
her that day. Upon reception of the word all
hands went to work to get everything in order.
Precisely at twelve o'clock she was prepared to
receive her guest. The house was as clean as a
pin; a sumptuous dinner was on the table, and
she was arrayed in her best attire. A gentle
knock was heard, and she started with a palpi-
tating heart to the door. She thought it must
be an old friend, perhaps a brother from the
place whence they had once moved. On opening
the door she saw her husband with a smiling
countenance.

"Why, my dear," said she in anxious tone,
"where is the gentleman of whom you spoke in
your note?"

"Why," replied the husband complacently,
"here he is."

"You said a gentleman of my acquaintance—
an old and true friend—would dine with us to-
day."

"Well," said he good humoredly, "am I not a
gentleman of your acquaintance, an old and true
friend?"

"Oh!" she cried distressingly, "is there no-
body but you?"

"No."

"Well, I declare this is too bad," said the wife
in a disappointed tone.

The husband laughed immoderately, and then
they both laughed, and finally they sat down
cosily together and enjoyed a good dinner, without having company, and they have done so many
times since.

In the following pages will be found a variety of practical recipes of incalculable value to the housewife, and no one can read them without being struck by the good sense which pervades them. It is amusing to notice the indefiniteness of most of the recipes which are floating through the newspapers. They presuppose experience and knowledge, and remind one of Dinah's recipe for making "delicious cornbread."

"Why, Darlin'," she said when asked how it was made, "sometimes gen'ally I takes a little meal, an' sometimes gen'ally I takes a little flour; an I kind o' mixes 'em with hot water; an' I puts in eggs 'nough, an' a little salt, an' then I bakes it just 'bout 'nough, an' you do so, jist so, honey, an' you'll make 'em good as I do." This is a fair sample of every day recipes, but care has been taken in those, here published, to make them intelligible to all. The superiority of Flavoring Extracts as a means of flavoring (and all cooking and pastry should be properly flavored) will be readily perceived by their use. Take Lemon for instance; by the use of the Extract the pure flavor alone is communicated; use the peel, and the bitter qualities are mingled, and often your pies or puddings are spoiled. In all things we should use the best means, for they are open to to all; a man may dig with a pitch fork, but is it the best instrument? It is important also that good Extracts be used, therefore ask your grocer or druggist for KNIGHTS' make, and take no other, and you may rest assured that you will get an article worthy of your confidence. See advertisement on the back cover of this book.

ICE CREAM.—Take one quart new milk, add when boiling, half a tablespoonful of arrowroot, wet with a little cold milk. When cold, add one pint of milk, half a pound of sugar, and one tablespoonful of Extract of Vanilla, or any other flavor you may desire; mix well together and place in a freezer; then place the freezer in a bucket and put broken ice and salt around it alternately so as to touch every part, and press it down tightly. Agitate the cream by turning the can back and forth with the hand; in about ten minutes open the can and stir in the portions that have adhered to the sides. Continue this until the whole is frozen into a stiff but smooth substance.

ANOTHER MADE WITH CREAM.—To one quart of rich cream, add one half pound of sugar and a small tablespoonful Extract Vanilla, or some other flavor if preferred, and proceed as above directed.

CREAM PUDDING.—Take one quart of milk, mix with two teaspoonsful Extract Nutmeg. Beat up the yolks of eight eggs with the whites of three, and mix with a dessertspoonful of flour, also with a quarter of a pound sweet almonds blanched and beaten fine with a teaspoonful of Extract Orange, then by degrees mix in the milk and beat all together; take a thick cloth, wet it, flour it well, pour in the mixture, tie it close and boil it half an hour, then turn it into a dish, pour melted butter over it and sprinkle fine sugar over all.

LEMON CAKE.—Mix ten ounces flour, five ounces butter, five ounces sugar; beat in the yolk of one egg, and flavor with two teaspoonsful Extract Lemon; divide into cakes and bake.

DEVONSHIRE CAKE.—Take one pound flour, one pound currants, three-quarter pounds sugar, half-pound butter, three teaspoonsful Extract Lemon, half pound citron, whisk all together with eight eggs, add a wineglassful brandy, and bake in a slow oven two hours and a half.

CUP CAKE.—Take five eggs, three cups sugar, one cup butter, four cups flour, one cup milk, one teaspoonful soda, one teaspoonful cream of Tartar, two teaspoonsful Extract Vanilla or Lemon; mix together and bake.

CREAM PIE.—Make a cake with one and a half cups sugar, one-third cup butter, three eggs, half cup milk, two and a half cups flour, one teaspoonful cream of Tartar, half teaspoonful soda, one teaspoonful Extract Nutmeg.

Make a filling with half cup flour, one cup sugar, two eggs beaten well together, and stirred into a pint of milk while boiling. When cool, flavor with two teaspoonsful Extract Vanilla or Lemon.

This is sufficient for two pies. Bake the cake in two loaves, cut them open and place the cream between.

---

Knight's Extracts, established in 1845.

PUFF CAKE.—Take two cups sugar, half cup butter, one cup milk, three cups flour, three eggs, half teaspoonful soda, one teaspoonful cream of Tartar, one teaspoonful Extract Vanilla or Orange. Bake in a quick oven.

LOVE CAKE.—Mix together three eggs, five ounces sugar, six ounces flour, a little salt, and a teaspoonful Extract Mace; to be dropped; sprinkle sugar on before baking.

APPLE TAPIOCA PUDDING.—Take four table-spoonsful of Tapioca, pour on a quart boiling water, let it boil until clear, then put in a table-spoonful of butter, when melted add four large apples, pared and sliced, sweeten to the taste, and add two teaspoonsful Extract Vanilla, Lemon or Orange; let it boil until the apples begin to soften, then bake in an oven half an hour. To be eaten cold with cream sweetened and flavored poured over it.

TAPIOCA BLANC MANGE.—Soak half a pound Tapioca for an hour in a pint of milk, boil till tender, sweeten to taste, and pour into a mould; serve with cream sweetened and flavored with Extract Vanilla or Strawberry.

SOLID CUSTARD.—Take one ounce isinglass, two pints new milk, the yolks of four eggs, sugar to taste; dissolve the isinglass in the milk, place upon the fire, let it boil a few minutes, add the yolks of the eggs well beaten, sweeten to the taste, and put it on the fire until it thickens, then remove and stir it until nearly cold, then stir in two teaspoonsful Extract Almonds, and place in a mould.

Flavor your cooking with Knight's Extracts.

# KNIGHT'S
## CELEBRATED PREMIUM CONCENTRATED
## FLAVORING EXTRACTS.

For flavoring Ice Creams, Jellies, Pies, Custards, Blanc Mange, Junket, Sauces, Soups, Gravies, Puddings, Cakes, and all fancy cooking.

These extracts were established in 1845, and an experience of nearly twenty-five years in their manufacture, warrants us in claiming for them *the first place* in the market. Their superiority consists in their great strength, perfect purity and delicacy of flavor, which is readily perceived by their use, being scientifically prepared by careful and experienced hands, from the choicest Fruits, Flowers, &c., and possessing their essential properties in the most concentrated form, free from all woody or inert substance, crude or bitter qualities, and the pure flavor alone being communicated.

The following are the flavors:

| | | | |
|---|---|---|---|
| Vanilla, | Lemon, | Strawberry, | Green Gage, |
| Ginger, | Cloves, | Jargonel Pear, | Allspice, |
| Almond, | Celery, | Nectarine, | Nutmeg, |
| Peach, | Mace, | Orange, | Pineapple, |
| Apricot, | Cinnamon, | Raspberry, | Rose. |

The above are not common *Essences*, but pure *Extracts*.

TRANSPARENT CUSTARDS.—Beat eight eggs very well, put them into a stew-pan with half pound of sugar pounded fine, and the same quantity of butter, to which add a teaspoonful Extract Nutmeg, set it on the fire, keep stirring it until it thickens, then set in a basin to cool; put a rich puff-paste round the sides of a dish, put in your custard, and bake in a moderate oven.

ECONOMICAL PUDDING.—Put two tablespoonsful of rice into a saucepan with as much water as the rice will absorb; when boiled enough, add a little salt, then set it by the fire until the rice is quite soft and dry; throw it up in a dish, add two ounces of butter, four tablespoonsful of Tapioca, one and a half pints of milk, sugar to taste, flavor with two teaspoonsful Extract Mace and two eggs beaten up. Stir well together, and bake an hour.

JUMBLES.—Rub to a cream one pound sugar, half pound butter, add eight well beaten eggs, two teaspoonsful Extract Lemon, flour enough to make the paste stiff enough to roll out; roll out in powdered sugar, about half an inch wide and four inches long, and form into rings. Lay on flat buttered tins, and bake in a quick oven.

STEAMED CUSTARDS.—Mix together four eggs, one pint milk, three tablespoonsful sugar, saltspoonful salt, and one and a half teaspoonful Extract Nutmeg. Steam fifteen to twenty minutes.

---

Knight's Extracts can be had of your grocer or druggist.

APPLE FRITTERS.—Pare and core some fine large pippins, cut them into round slices, soak them for two or three hours in wine sweetened, and sufficient Extract Nutmeg to flavor. Make a batter of four eggs, a teaspoonful Extract Rose, a tablespoonful wine, a tablespoonful milk, thicken with enough flour stirred in by degrees to make a batter, mix it two or three hours before you want it, so that it may be light; dip each slice of apple in the batter, and fry them in butter; when done, sift powdered sugar on them.

APPLE SNOW.—Pare and core twelve apples, steam them until tender, set the apples aside to cool, then put over them a whip made of the whites of three eggs beaten to a stiff froth. Serve with sugar and cream flavored with Extract Vanilla.

MOSS BLANC MANGE.—Take as much Irish moss as will fill a coffee cup, put it into a bowl and pour boiling water over it, and let it stand about ten minutes, wash it out and soak it over night in cold water; put the water and moss into three quarts of milk the next morning, and boil ten minutes, strain it through a very fine sieve or muslin into moulds, add half a teaspoonful salt. Serve with sugar and cream flavored with Extract Vanilla, Lemon or Strawberry.

RICE PUDDING.—Take one cup of rice, one quart milk, sugar to taste, a tablespoonful of butter, two eggs, quarter pound of raisins, and two teaspoonsful Extract Vanilla; mix together, let it come to a boil, and then place in the oven to bake.

Buy no Extracts but Knight's.

OXFORD DUMPLINGS.—Mix well together two ounces grated bread, four ounces currants, four ounces suet, one tablespoonful sifted' sugar, a teaspoonful Extract Allspice, two teaspoonsful Extract Lemon, two eggs well beaten, and sufficient milk to make the proper consistence, and divide the mixture into five dumplings; fry them in butter a light brown color, and serve with wine sauce.

FLOATING ISLAND.—Beat the whites of five eggs with a little currant jelly until they are quite thick and of a good color, drop them by spoonsful into a dish; sweeten a pint cream, add one teaspoonful Extract Rose, and pour the cream in gently around these islands.

GOLD CAKE.—Beat half cup of butter to a cream, add a cup and a half sugar, then the yolks of three eggs well beaten, then two cups flour; dissolve half a teaspoonful soda, half a teaspoonful cream of Tartar, a little salt, and a teaspoonful Extract Vanilla in half a cup milk, then stir all together just before placing in the oven.

SILVER CAKE.—Make the same as above, substituting the whites of three eggs for the yolks. Extract Pineapple, Rose, or any other flavor, may be used.

RAISED DOUGHNUTS.—Mix together one pint milk, three eggs, one cup sugar, one cup molasses, one cup yeast, half cup butter, one teaspoonful soda, two teaspoonsful salt, and two teaspoonsful Extract Allspice; form into doughnuts and bake.

Try Knight's Extracts, and be con-

## EXTRACT VANILLA.

This delightful flavor, which is so well known and so much admired, because of its general use in the flavor of Ice Cream, is manufactured from the bean of the " Vanilla Aromatica," a plant of peculiar growth, the best varieties of which we receive from Mexico; it is a climbing, shrubby, ærial plant, which commences its growth in the crevices of rocks, or on the trunks of trees, suspending itself to contiguous objects, and finally becomes detached from the original support, being truly an ærial plant. Our agent in Mexico gives us some interesting accounts of the mode of preparing the fruit or beans for market, which, however, our space will not permit us to publish here. Our preparation of Vanilla possesses the peculiar flavor of the fruit to a great degree, and readily communicates its properties to pastry and fancy cooking generally.

*Directions for Use.*—When it is possible it should be added after the article is removed from the fire, and be thoroughly stirred in while cooling. The quantity used should be governed by the taste—usually about a teaspoonful to the pint. For acid sauces, as apples, &c., it is better to mix cold a short time before using. If mixed while hot, the quantity must be increased, as a great portion of the strength is evaporated or lost.

In purchasing, be sure to get Knight's Extracts, for there are many worthless articles in the market.

SUGAR DOUGHNUTS.—Dissolve one teaspoonful of soda in two-thirds of a cup of milk, then add three eggs, one and a half cups sugar, and two teaspoonsful butter well beaten together; add to the mixture as much flour as will make it stiff enough to roll; a little salt and a teaspoonful Extract Nutmeg should be added to the milk.

SPONGE CAKE.—Take three eggs, one cup sugar, one and a half cups of flour, seven tablespoonsful milk, a little salt, half teaspoonful soda, half teaspoonful cream of Tartar, one teaspoonful Extract Lemon; beat all together and bake.

COCOA-NUT PUDDING.—Melt two ounces butter, stir in two ounces sugar, boil up for a moment, when cool grate in two ounces cocoa-nut, and two ounces shred citron, one teaspoonful Extract Lemon, and four eggs well beaten; put into cups and bake half an hour, or in one large dish and bake longer.

COTTAGE PUDDING.—Three cups flour, one cup sugar, one cup milk, two tablespoonsful butter, two teaspoonsful cream of Tartar, one egg; beat all well together, then add one teaspoonful soda, and one teaspoonful Extract Lemon; bake one half hour; serve with sauce made in the following manner:

Sauce—one cup butter, two cups powdered sugar, beaten to a cream; then add half pint boiling water, and when cool, add two tablespoonsful wine, and one teaspoonful Extract Vanilla.

---

Take no Extracts but Knight's, when you buy, and thus avoid all worthless articles.

POTATO PUDDINGS.—Boil three large potatoes, mash smooth with one ounce butter, three ounces thick cream, add three eggs beaten, a teaspoonful brown sugar, a pinch of salt, and a teaspoonful Extract Nutmeg; beat all well together, and bake in a buttered dish, thirty minutes, in a quick oven.

SMALL COLD PUDDING.—Into a pint of new milk, beat the yolks of six eggs, sweeten to taste, and add two teaspoonsful Extract Pineapple; pour the mixture into cups, steam for half an hour, next day turn out and garnish with jelly.

A QUICK MADE PUDDING.—One pound flour, one pound suet, quarter pint new milk, two teaspoonsful Extract Mace, half pound raisins, quarter pound currants; mix well and boil three quarters of an hour in a floured cloth.

MARLBOROUGH TARTS.—Quarter and stew very tender, juicy apples; to a teacupful of the pulp, rubbed through a sieve, put the same measure of sugar, same of wine, half a teacupful melted butter, two teaspoonsful Extract Raspberry, a tumblerful of milk, four eggs, two teaspoonsful Extract Nutmeg; mix all well together, turn into a deep pie-plate lined with pastry. Bake about thirty minutes.

SUET PUDDING.—Take four cups flour, one cup molasses, one cup suet, one cup milk, one cup raisins, one teaspoonful soda, two teaspoonsful Extract Mace, mix, and boil three hours.

---

Knight's Extracts are made from the fruits at the season when the purest flavor may be extracted.

LEMON TART.—Mix together the yolks of twelve eggs, twelve ounces sugar, twelve ounces butter, the whites of six eggs, one tablespoonful Extract Lemon; bake in plates the bottom lined with paste.

LEMON PIE.—Take one lemon, one cup sugar, yolk of two eggs, half cup milk, half cup water, half a cracker, two teaspoonsful butter; place in a crust made in the usual way, and bake in a quick oven; when done beat the whites of the above eggs with one teaspoonful Extract Lemon to a stiff froth, spread over your pie, sprinkle sugar over it and brown it.

POP OVERS.—Stir three eggs, three cups flour, three cups milk, one teaspoonful Extract Orange to a smooth batter, and bake in cups.

AMALGAMATION CAKE.—Mix together the whites of eight eggs, three cups sugar, one cup butter, five cups flour, one teaspoonful soda, one teaspoonful cream of Tartar, and two teaspoonsful Extract Lemon. Then take the yolks of the above eight eggs, two cups brown sugar, one cup molasses, one cup butter, one cup buttermilk, one tablespoonful soda, one egg, two teaspoonsful each, Extract Cloves, Extract Allspice, and Extract Cinnamon; mix together. Put alternately a layer of each mixture in a baking dish and bake in a quick oven.

WASHINGTON CAKE.—Five cups sifted flour, three cups sugar, half cup butter, three gills milk, quarter pound each raisins, citron, and currants, three eggs, small teaspoonful soda; one teaspoonful each, Extracts Pineapple, Strawberry and Nutmeg; mix together and bake.

---

The best fruits only are used in Knight's Extracts.

# EXTRACT OF LEMON.

This flavor is used probably more than any other except Vanilla, and is deservedly a very popular flavoring agent. It is procured from the lemons which come principally from Messina. Our Extract of Lemon is prepared with great care, and is recommended as a flavor which will retain its sweetness for any length of time, being on this account much superior to the oil or the ordinary essences, which are so common in the market, and which are liable to become rancid by age. It is so purified and concentrated, that a few drops possesses the strength of a lemon, and can be used at any season of the year, even when the fruit cannot be obtained, and is really much cheaper. As an addition to pastry, cooking, ice cream, jellies, &c., this flavor will be found invaluable, used according to the directions given for Extract Vanilla.

---

# EXTRACT OF CELERY.

This Extract possesses the peculiar flavor of the plant to a great degree, and may be used whenever that flavor may be desired. To chicken salad it proves a most excellent addition. It may also be added to soups, gravies, &c.

---

In one dozen bottles of Knight's Extracts, is condensed the flavor of a bushel of fruit.

JELLY MADE WITHOUT FRUIT.—To one package of Cox's Refined Gelatine, add one pint of cold water; let it stand one hour; then add three pints boiling water, two pounds sugar, boil and add two teaspoonsful Tartaric acid, one pint Sherry or Madeira wine, one tablespoonful Extract Orange, and one tablespoonful Extract Lemon, or other flavors if desired, and strain through a flannel bag into moulds or into ordinary dishes as may be desired; set it in a cold place and let it stand for several hours. This will make about three quarts. In warm weather less water should be used.

CELERY SAUCE.—Boil an onion in half a pint of water, when tender, add salt and pepper, a gill of milk, and thicken with pounded cracker; boil it a quarter of an hour, and then pass it through a sieve with the back of a spoon; when done add three teaspoonsful Extract Celery.

VEGETABLE SOUP.—One onion, two turnips, one carrot, one quart of water, sufficient salt and half tablespoonful of butter braided in flour; make into soup, and when removed from the fire, add two teaspoonsful Extract Celery, one teaspoonful Extract Cloves, one teaspoonful Extract Mace.

FANCY FLAVORS.—By a combination of two or more of Knight's Extracts, a variety of new flavors may be produced.

---

Many suffering sick have blessed the day when they discovered Knight's Cooking Extracts.

APPLE BREAD PUDDING.—Pare, core and stew six large apples and a large tablespoonful of butter, sweeten to the taste, and add two teaspoonsful Extract Pineapple. Then line the bottom of a pudding dish with bread crumbs and place in alternate layers of apples and bread crumbs until your dish is full, sprinkle sugar on the top, add a tablespoonful of butter and bake. To be eaten cold with milk, sweetened and flavored with Extract Lemon, poured over it.

APPLE SAUCE.—Pare, core and stew four large apples, sweeten to taste, and stir in two teaspoonsful butter, when cold, add one teaspoonful Extract of Rose or Lemon.

USE OF FLAVORS.—Housekeepers who have private recipes will find upon trial that the addition of flavoring Extracts to them will greatly improve their quality.

FRUIT CAKE.—Sugar, butter and flour one pound each, ten eggs, currants two pounds, raisins two pounds, stoned and chopped fine, one half pound citron, half tumbler of brandy, in which the currants and raisins must be rinsed to prevent them settling at the bottom of the cake. Work the butter to a cream, and rub the sugar well in, then gradually the flour ; beat the yolks and whites of the eggs separately, then mix all together; then add the brandy and fruit, two teaspoonsful Extract Mace and two teaspoonsful Extract Cinnamon or Lemon.

---

Twenty-five years' experience, has brought Knight's Extracts to perfection.

PLEASANT BEVERAGES.—Take three table-spoonsful of syrup made as directed below, of whichever flavor is desired; place into a tumbler and fill with ice water, mix thoroughly together. These will be found to be very pleasant drinks, the syrup being much superior to those made to sell in the stores. To create a foam, if it be desired, add half a teaspoonful of baking soda dissolved in a little water.

SYRUP OF STRAWBERRY.—Dissolve one tea-spoonful Tartaric acid in half a pint water, then add one pound white sugar, and place over the fire, stirring it until the sugar is dissolved; strain, and when cold, add one tablespoonful Extract of Strawberry, and mix thoroughly together.

SYRUP OF RASPBERRY.—Make as above, substituting Extract of Raspberry for Strawberry.

SYRUP PINEAPPLE.—Make in the same way, using Extract Pineapple.

SYRUP BANANA.—Make in the same way, using Extract Banana.

In the same way may be made Syrups of Vanilla, Apricot, Lemon, Jargonel Pear, Nectarine, Orange, and Green Gage.

RASPBERRY VINEGAR.—Take the Raspberry Syrup made as above, and add to one pint of it a tablespoonful of vinegar, and mix well together.

---

Ladies who use Knight's Extracts, wonder how they got along without them.

## Extract of Strawberry,
## " Raspberry.
## " Pineapple,
## " Jargonel Pear.

These fruit Extracts may be used whenever he flavor of the fruits which they represent is lesired. They are manufactured in such manner, and so highly concentrated, that a small rial represents as much strength as a quart of he juice. A teaspoonful added to the pint of he article to be flavored will be about the proper proportion if added when cool. They are well adapted for Ice Creams, Jellies, Puddings, Syrups, &c.

——:o:——

## Extract of Bitter Almonds,
## " Peach.

These extracts are used most generally for lavoring cakes, being better adapted for this purpose than for jellies and sauces. Their flavor is too well known to require comment here, and by using KNIGHT'S EXTRACTS he true flavor may be communicated as desired. About a teaspoonful to the pound of cake is the proportion generally used, but persons may lavor to suit their tastes, which will be readily ascertained by trial.

---

Knight's Extracts have been in use twenty-five years, and all who have used them speak well of them.

CREAM MARANGE.—A custard made of one pint of milk and four eggs, leaving out the whites of two; one tablespoonful Extract Vanilla, two teaspoonsful Extract Rose; make it very sweet; dissolve one ounce of isinglass, and stir into the custard; beat to a froth one pint of rich cream, and when the custard is mixed with the isinglass, pour it over the frothed cream, stirring it well. Fix lady-fingers cakes or slices of sponge cake in the mould, and when the mixtuae is cool, pour it in and set it on ice till served. If, when all mixed, the custard does not seem frothy, churn well with a whip-stick till it does, before putting it into the mould. The isinglass should be kept warm while the custard thickens, and then added. You may make a richer custard with ten eggs, leaving out the whites of six. With the whites you may make the snow.

APPLE PIE WITHOUT APPLES.—Grate two teaspoonsful of bread crumbs, take sufficient water to moisten thoroughly, a teaspoonful of Tartaric acid, sweeten to taste, mix well together, and let it come to a boil; when cool, add two teaspoonsful Extract Nutmeg and one teaspoonful Extract Lemon; then make your pie and use the above as you would stewed apples. This will make a pie that any one would pronounce a good apple pie.

---

Nutmeg graters are rendered obsolete by the use of Knight's Extracts.

HUCKLEBERRY PUDDING.—Make a paste with one quart of flour and half a pound of butter; rub one half the butter into the flour; mix this with cold water; roll it out and put on the remainder of the butter in little pieces; roll it out half an inch thick, spread the cloth previously dipped in water and well floured over the colander; lay the paste on it; fill it with berries; tie the cloth tight; put it into boiling water and boil two hours. Serve with sweetened cream flavored with Extract Jargonel Pear or Extract Strawberry.

PUMPKIN PIES.—To nine tablespoonsful of strained pumpkin add one quart of boiled milk, four eggs, a little salt, three tablespoonsful of wine, one teaspoonful Extract of Rose, one teaspoonful Extract Lemon, half teaspoonful Tararic acid; sweeten to taste, and make into pies.

CALVES' FOOT JELLY.—Take four feet and boil them in one gallon of water to two quarts; strain t to cool, and when cold take off the fat; put the jelly on the fire with one pint and a half gill of wine and one gill of brandy; one pound of loaf sugar, one teaspoonful Tartaric acid, one teaspoonful Extract Lemon, the whites of seven eggs with the shells. Boil all together for one half hour, then pass it through a thick flannel bag until clear.

---

Numerous testimonials could be shown in favor of Knight's Extracts, but their best recommendation is their use.

SYRUP OF GINGER.—Take half a pint of water and add one pound of white sugar; place it over the fire and stir until the sugar is dissolved; strain, and when it is cold, add Extract of Ginger to the taste, stirring it well together.

GINGERBREAD.—Take two cups sugar, one cup butter, one cup sour milk, two cups flour, one teaspoonful soda, three eggs, and two teaspoonsful Extract Ginger, mix well together; and bake.

GINGER SNAPS.—Two and a half pounds of flour, half pound of butter or lard, half a pound of sugar, one pint molasses, one teaspoonful saleratus, two teaspoonsful Extract Ginger. This should be rolled very thin and baked but a few minutes. It softens by being kept.

SPONGE GINGERBREAD.—Two tablespoonsful of butter, two cups molasses, one cup milk, one teaspoonful soda, flour to make a pretty stiff batter, two teaspoonsful Extract Ginger.

EXCELLENT SUMMER DRINK.—To prevent cramp in the stomach, or such complaints which are so common in warm weather, take a tablespoonful Syrup of Ginger, a teaspoonful of Extract Ginger, a tumblerful of water, and drink during the day.

Grocers keep Knight's Extracts.

## Extract of Rose,
## " Orange.

These extracts represent the true flavors of the flowers and fruit from which they are obtained, and may be used for all culinary purposes the same as Extract of Lemon.

——:o:——

## Extract Ginger.

This Extract, so generally known and esteemed for its valuable medicinal properties and uses, is also capable of being advantageously used for culinary purposes, being made from the purest Jamaica Root in a very concentrated form. Syrup Ginger, made as on the previous page, makes a pleasant beverage when added to water. For making Ginger Cake, its use is far superior and much more convenient than the powdered, root, as the latter article varies very much on account of age and the impurities frequently found in it, whereas the extract is always of uniform strength. As a medicine, it will be found a valuable remedy in cases of Dyspepsia, Flatulency, Cholic, Cholera Morbus, Nausea, Sea Sickness, Cramps or Pain in the Stomach, Diarrhea, Gout, Rheumatism, Weakness, Debility, &c.

Dose for an adult—From one-half to one teaspoonful, to be taken in sweetened water. For children in proper proportion.

Knight's Extract of Ginger may be used as a medicine or as a flavor.

PUMPKIN CUSTARD.—Take five pounds pumpkin, pare off the outside rind, discard it, then divide into slices, take three or four good-sized apples cut into small pieces, and put the pumpkin and apples together in a deep dish, adding one and a half pounds of moist sugar, two teaspoonsful each Extracts Allspice, Cloves and Lemon, a teacupful sweet cider; mix together, cover the dish over with a thick, plain paste, bake in a steady oven for one hour.

SPANISH BISCUIT.—Beat the yolks of eight eggs nearly one half hour, then beat in eight tablespoonsful of white sugar, then beat the whites of the eggs to a strong froth, then mix all well together, add four tablespoonsful of flour and two teaspoonsful Extract of Cinnamon, divide into biscuits, and bake on papers.

TOMATO CATCHUP.—Skin, slice, and boil the tomatoes well; then put to one gallon not strained one ounce of scraped horseradish and one teaspoonful Cayenne pepper, and salt to your taste; boil this away to three quarts, and strain; then add a pint of wine, half a pint of vinegar, one tablespoonful each Extracts Mace, Nutmegs and Cloves, mix well together. Bottle it and leave the bottles open two or three days, as it sometimes ferments a little, and requires scalding; then cork tightly.

---

Housekeepers who have become disgusted with common Extracts, are requested to try Knight's make.

RYE PAN CAKES.—Prepare the lard as you would to fry doughnuts; take one tumblerful of milk, one of syrup or light molasses, piece of butter the size of a walnut, two teaspoonsful Extract Mace, one teaspoonful of soda, one egg, and a little salt. Put the soda with the milk, add the syrup, then the Extract of Mace, butter, salt and eggs, stir into this the rye until you have a rather stiff batter, then take another spoon, dip it into the hot lard, then take of the rye batter a piece about the size of an English walnut, and fry. By dipping the spoon into the hot lard the batter will drop nicely into the lard without scraggling. As it takes sometime to cook them through, the lard or fire should not be too hot. Eat with sauce flavored with Extract Vanilla.

LEMON JELLY.—Take one box Cox's Refined Gelatine, pour over it one quart boiling water, stir until all is dissolved, add a teaspoonful Tartaric acid, four cups sugar; when it is all dissolved, add the whites of four eggs well beaten, and let it boil up once over the fire, add two teaspoonsful Extract Lemon ; strain into moulds **or** cups, and let it stand until stiff.

GOOD RECIPE FOR DIGESTION:

"After dinner, rest awhile;
After supper, walk a mile."

Knight's Extracts are put up in two ounce bottles.

GRAHAM BREAD.—Take one coffee-cup of white flour, two of Graham flour, one of warm water, half a cup of yeast, and a little molasses, a small teaspoonful of salt, and half a teaspoonful of saleratus dissolved in the water. It should be made as stiff as can be stirred with a spoon. If you prefer to add a spoonful of Indian meal it should be scalded. Let it rise over night, and when it is very light bake it about an hour in a moderate heat. The above recipe will make one loaf of bread.

HAM TOAST.—This is very convenient to hand round with chicken or with roast veal, and also makes a tasty breakfast or luncheon dish. Mince very finely the lean of a slice or two of boiled ham, beat the yolks of two eggs and mix them with ham, adding as much cream or stock as will make it soft; keep it long enough on the fire to warm it through—it may be allowed almost to boil, but should be stirred all the time. Have ready some buttered toast, cut it in round pieces, and lay the ham neatly on each piece.

SUPERIOR JOHNNY CAKE.—Two eggs, half a cup of molasses, half cup of sugar, half cup butter, one pint butter milk, one teaspoonful saleratus, a little salt, one teaspoonful Extract Allspice; make a batter with two-thirds meal and one-third flour. To be eaten warm, with butter.

Knight's Extracts are unsurpassed for purity and strength.

Extract of Nutmeg,
"           Cinnamon,
"           Cloves,
"           Allspice,
"           Mace.

These Extracts, manufactured from the purest spices bearing their names, are of first quality, and are much more convenient than the powders bearing the same names, as the latter are frequently inert and worthless from age or inferiority of quality, or adulterations with which they are mixed, while the Extracts will retain their strength and purity for any length of time, and in any climate. These Extracts are much more desirable for spicing fish, pickles, &c., than the whole or powdered spices, because the flavor of one is communicated without the woody portions. Extract of Nutmeg is much better for flavoring custards, &c., than the grated nutmeg, for it mingles with the whole custard, whereas the Nutmeg itself always rises to the top.

——:o:——

Extract of Apricot,
"           Green Gage,
"           Nectarine.

These Extracts, though not so well known as any others, are nevertheless very much admired by those who have used them. They may be used whenever a fruit flavor is desired.

Knight's flavors are excelled by none.

WINTER DINNER.—Soup, Roast Beef, Stewed Onions, Cold Slaw, Turnips, Apple Sauce, Apple Pie and Custard.

ANOTHER.—Boiled Ham, Oyster Pie, Turnips, Potatoes, Parsnips, Baked Rice Puddings and Preserved Tomatoes.

ANOTHER.—Bean Soup, Roast Pork with Apple Sauce, Turnips, Potatoes, Beets, Pumpkin Pudding, Preserved Plums.

A FINE DINNER.—Chicken Pot-pie, Oyster Fritters, Turnips, Parsnips, Beets, Cold Slaw, Plum Pudding, Preserved Peaches.

CHRISTMAS DINNER.—Roast Turkey, Cranberry Sauce, Boiled Fowls with Celery Sauce, Boiled Ham, Goose Pie, Turnips, Cold Slaw, Squash, Beets, Hominy, Mince Pie, Boiled Lemon Pudding and Baked Pumpkin Pudding.

NEW YEAR'S DINNER.—Boiled Turkey, with Oyster Sauce; Roast Goose, with Apple Sauce; Boiled Tongue, Chicken Pie, Stewed Beets, Cold Slaw, Sweet and White Potatoes, Turnips, Winter Squash, Mince Pie, Plum Pudding, Lemon Custard, Cranberry Tart.

AN EXCELLENT DINNER.—Venison Soup, Roast Fowls, Stewed Beets, Sweet Potatoes, Turnips, Squash, Sago Pudding, and Baked Apples.

BOILED DINNER.—Boiled Corn Beef, Cabbage, Carrots, Parsnips, Potatoes, Turnips, Apple Pie and Boiled Custard.

---

Ask your storekeeper for Knight's Extracts.

The undersigned, having formerly been en-aged in the manufacture and sale of COOKING nd FLAVORING EXTRACTS, in the city of hiladelphia, and having parted with my ntire interest in the business, take pleasure 1 informing the public that my successors, [ESSRS. RICHARDS, WARREN & FLINT BRO's, t No. 69 North Second Street, Philadelphia, ave now the exclusive control of the business, nd are manufacturing the same quality of lavors under the name of KNIGHT's COOKING XTRACTS, from the original recipes formerly sed by me, and so favorably known in the 1arket for the last twenty-five years.

I cheerfully recommend them to my old ·iends as gentlemen entitled to their confidence nd patronage.

CHAS D. KNIGHT

HILAD'A, June 16th, 1869.

☞ HOUSEKEEPERS who have never used **KNIGHT'S FLAVORING EXTRACTS**. should certainly make a trial of them, to discover their rich quality, and the great improvement they are to cooking and pastry. Those who do not use them because they have never *seen* the benefit of them, are like old Major Foughy, who was opposed to the magnetic telegraph before its introduction. He fought against it with all his power, yet in the progress of events, the poles were raised, and the wires were stretched, and the Major was called upon to behold the improvement. "I tell you, gentlemen," said he, "I have given my attention to this thing, and it will never work; it may do for letters and *small packages*, but for large parcels it is not worth a darn."

————:o:————

## YOU CAN GET

# KNIGHT'S EXTRACTS

## From Your Storekeeper.

☞ *See advertisement on the cover of this book.*

# THE INCREASING DEMAND FOR

# Cooking Extracts

has caused the production of inferior articles by various parties, and the effect of such preparations in the market has been to injure the sale of reliable Extracts, because people become disappointed in their use.

We have studied to preserve the standard quality of our Extracts by availing ourselves of all improvements in their manufacture, and the result has been that we have been gratified by a steady increase in our business.

To those who have not used Knight's Extracts we would say,

## PLEASE MAKE A TRIAL OF THEM

and be convinced of their superiority.

## RICHARDS, WARREN & FLINT BRO'S.

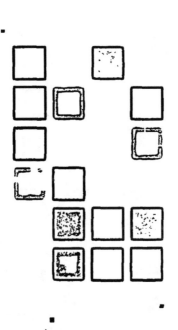

CPSIA information can be obtained
at www.ICGtesting.com
Printed in the USA
LVHW020132030523
745960LV00002B/67

9 781363 762361